LOVE IS WHEN YOU MEET A MAN WHO DOESN'T LIVE WITH HIS MOTHER

♥

BY IRENE PACHANIK

ILLUSTRATED BY ED POWERS • DESIGNED BY BERNARD NAGLER

PRICE STERN SLOAN publishers, INC.

LOS ANGELES

Love is when you meet a man who doesn't live with his mother

Love is when
the seat belt in his
car hasn't been
adjusted since
the last time
you used
it

LOVE IS WHEN
HE DOESN'T TAKE
THE PHONE
INTO THE NEXT
ROOM IF IT RINGS
WHEN YOU'RE
IN HIS
APARTMENT

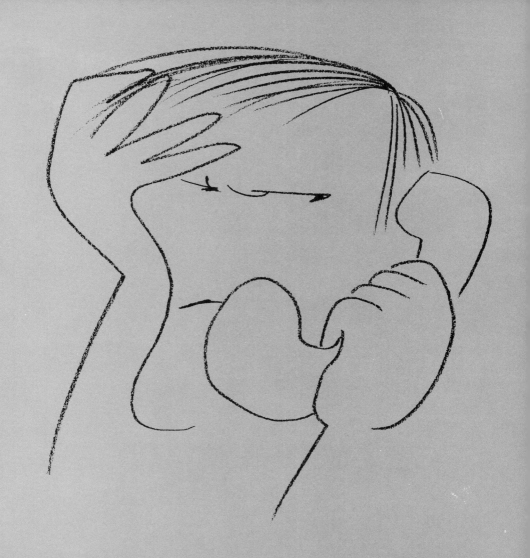

LOVE
IS WHEN
HE
COMES BACK
FOR A SECOND DATE
AFTER YOU'VE SAID
"NO"
THE FIRST TIME

Love is when
he comes back for a second date
after you've said

the first time

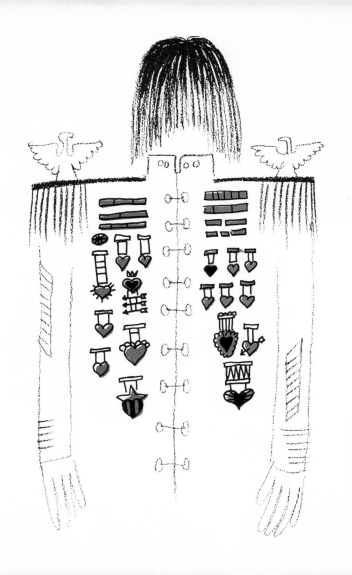

Love is when
he's still interested in you
after he finds out
your mother has an accent
(not French)

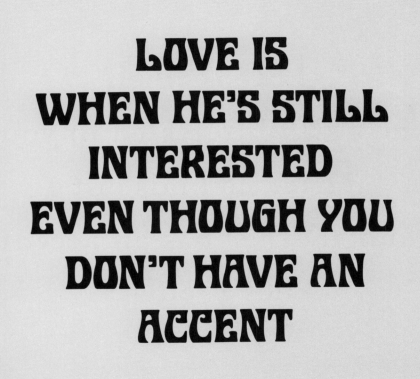

LOVE IS
WHEN HE'S STILL
INTERESTED
EVEN THOUGH YOU
DON'T HAVE AN
ACCENT

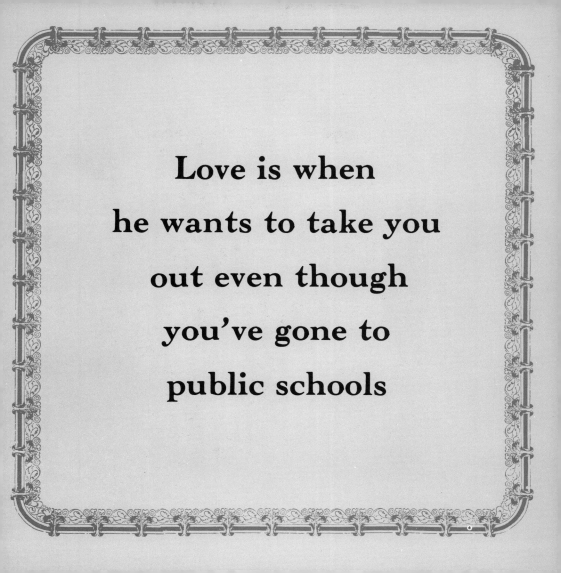

Love is when
he wants to take you
out even though
you've gone to
public schools

LOVE IS WHEN

HE SAYS

"I'LL CALL YOU

TOMORROW NIGHT"

—AND DOES!

Love is when
he "explores the mysteries"
of that
swinging foreign girl
and comes back to you

Love is when
you know where he is
on the nights
he's not with you

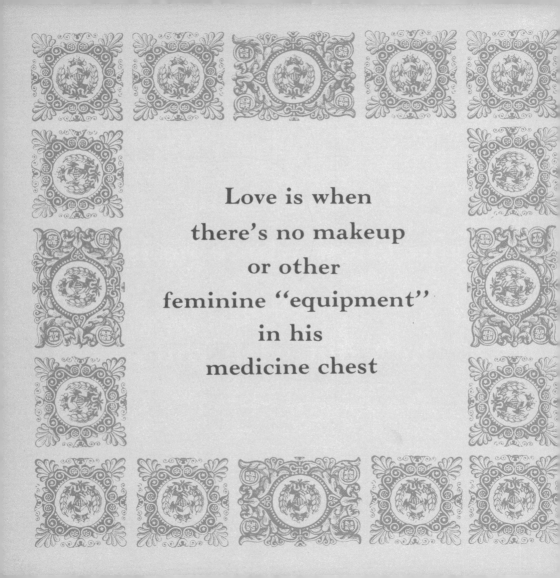

Love is when
there's no makeup
or other
feminine "equipment"
in his
medicine chest

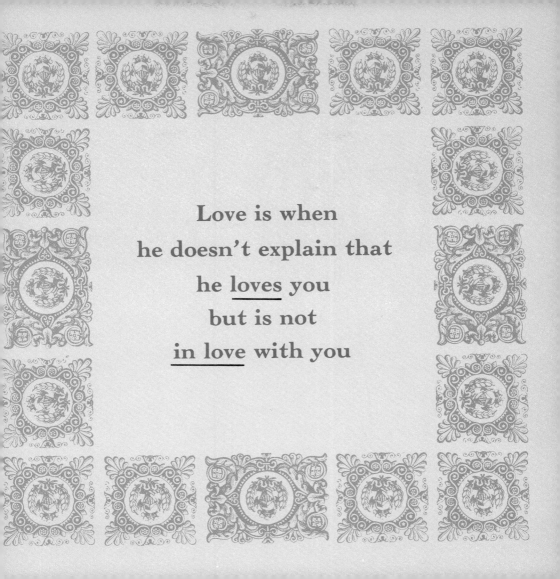

Love is when
he doesn't explain that
he <u>loves</u> you
but is not
<u>in love</u> with you

Love is when
he puts his arm
around you
the first time you meet
his mother

* is when he gives you a

personal gift on your birthday

—instead of something for your apartment

Love
he doesn't nee
to himself
taking y
Saturo

when
Friday night
cause he's
u out on
y night

Love is when
he doesn't need
Sunday afternoon
to himself
after seeing you
Saturday night

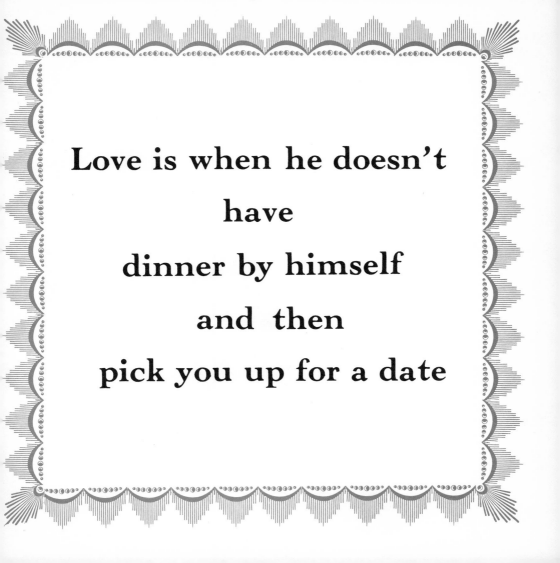

Love is when he doesn't

have

dinner by himself

and then

pick you up for a date

Love is when
he doesn't get pale and sick
if his friends think
there might be
"something between you"

Love is when he doesn't put off calling

after making love to you.

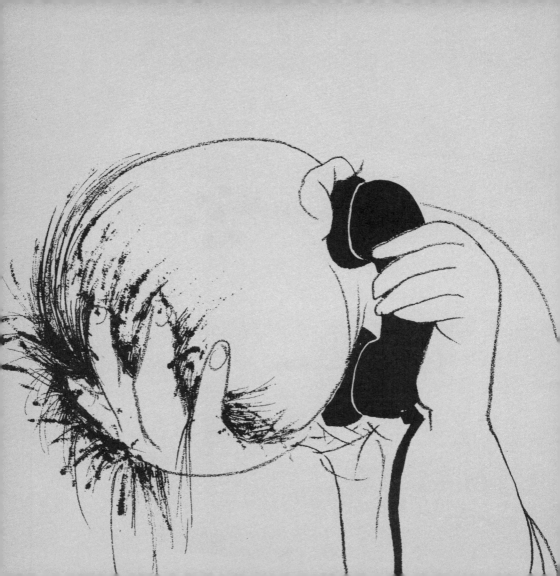

Love
is when he doesn't sound
awkward and strained
if you phone him
after
he's made love to you

Love is when
he doesn't
let on to his friends
that you are having
an affair

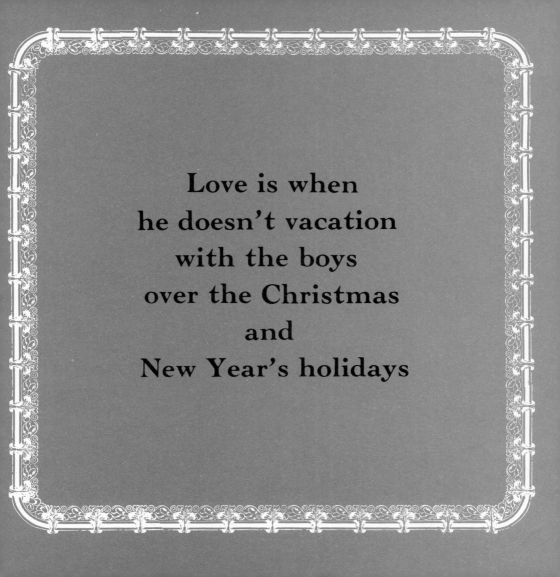

Love is when
he doesn't vacation
with the boys
over the Christmas
and
New Year's holidays

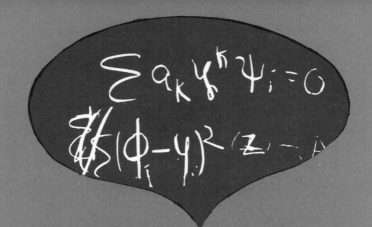

LOVE IS WHEN

YOUR SEX APPEAL

REACHES HIM

IN SPITE

OF YOUR INTELLIGENCE

Love is when he's had his fill of post-divorce affairs by
the time he's met you.

Love is when he doesn't insist on knowing
about every romance you had before you met him.

Love is when
he doesn't say
you remind him
of his first wife

THEATER DIR

BEST MUSICAL 1965-NY DRAMA CRITICS AND 9 TONY AWARDS

HERSCHEL BERNARDI in FIDDLER ON THE ROOF

WORLD'S MOST ACCLAIMED MUSICAL

also starring MARIA KARNILOVA

Directed by JEROME ROBBINS

PRICES: Mon.-Sat. Evgs.: Orch. & Boxes $9.90; Front Mezz. $8.50; Rear Mezz. $8.00, 7.00, 6.40, 5.40, 4.60. Wed. Mat.: Orch. & Boxes $5.80; Front Mezz. $5.10; Rear Mezz. $4.60, 4.00, 3.60, 2.80. Sat. & Sept. 5 Mat.: Orch. & Boxes $6.10; Front Mezz. $5.50; Rear Mezz. $5.10, 4.60, 4.00, 3.60. Enclose self-addressed, stamped envelope. List alternate dates.
Air-Cond. IMPERIAL, W. 45th St. 265-2412

AMERICA'S GREATEST MUSICAL HIT! GINGER ROGERS in HELLO, DOLLY!

Directed & Choreographed by GOWER CHAMPION

MAIL ORDERS FILLED. All Evgs.: $9.90, 8.05, 7.50, 6.90, 5.75, 4.80, 3.60. Mats. Wed. & Sat.: $6.25, 5.50, 4.80, 4.30, 3.80, 3.00.
Air-Cond. ST. JAMES, W. 44th St. 695-5858

MAIL ORDERS NOW OPENS THURS. EVG. SEPT. 29

Previews Sept. 26, 27, 28

HELP STAMP OUT MARRIAGE!

A Comedy By
KEITH WATERHOUSE and WILLIS HALL
Directed by GEORGE ABBOTT

Roddy   Ann   Francis   Valerie
Maude-Roxby Bell   Matthews   French
Evgs. Mon. thru Sat.: Orch. $7.50; Mezz. $6.90, 5.75, 4.80, 3.60, 3. Mats. Wed. & Sat.: Orch. $5.75; Mezz. $5.25, 4.80, 4.00, 3.60.
BOOTH THEATRE 222 W. 45TH ST. N.Y.C.

MAIL ORDERS NOW—OPENS MON. OCT. 24 14 POPULAR PRICED PREVIEWS—
OCT. 12 thru OCT. 22. Mats. Oct. 12, 15, 19, 22. Evgs. Oct. 12, 13, 14, 15, 17, 18, 19, 20, 21, 22. Mon. thru Sat. Evgs. Orch. $5. Balc. $4.25, 3. Wed. & Sat. Mats. Orch. $4.25. Balc. $3.50, 2.25.

HOW'S THE WORLD TREATING YOU?

"FUNNIEST PLAY OF 1966!"
—London Daily Express
MUSIC BOX THEA. 239 W. 45th St. N.Y.C.

"BROADWAY'S BEST MUSICAL!"
—Life Magazine
"A LOVELY HIT!"
—Lewis, Cue

ANGELA LANSBURY as MAME

The New Smash Hit Musical
Evgs. at 8:30: Orch. $9.50 (beg. Jan. 1 $9.90); Loge $9.00; Front Mezz. $8.50; Rear Mezz. $7.50, 6.50. Mats. Wed. at 2 & Sat. at 2:30: Orch. $6.25; Loge $5.75; Front Mezz. $5.25; Rear Mezz. $4.25, 3.25. List alt. dates.
Air-Cd. WINTER GARDEN, B'y&50St.245-4878

MAT. TODAY & EVERY S
BEST MUSICAL - 1966 - AL
N. Y. CRITICS AWA
TONY AWARD
OUTER CIRCLE AW
RICHARD KILE
IRVING   RAY
JACOBSON   MIDDLETON
JOAN DIENER
MAN OF La M
A New Musical Pl
Seats Available Beg. Nov. 1.
thru Sat. at 8:30: $8.50, 7.50
Mats. Wed. at 2: $5.50, 4.75, 3
& Sun. at 2:30: $6, 5.50, 4, 3.
Air-Cond. ANTA WASHINGT
(30 W. 4th St. bet. Wash. S
BOX OFFICE OPEN Mon. thru
Til 9 P.M.; Sun. 12 P.M. 'Til
For Ticket Info: 671-5600. A
Tickets Also at Shubert Alley

"A FINE AND POIGNAN
MOVING AND BEAUTIFUL
PHILADELPHIA, HERE I C
A New Comedy
MAIL ORDERS FILLED: Evg
5.50, 4.60, 3.90, 3.45, 2.80. Ma
$4.80, 3.90, 3.45, 2.80, 2.20.
Air-Cd. Helen Hayes, 210 W. 4
Moves Oct. 3 to Plymouth Th

"A GROOVY MUSICAL SPAR
GWEN VERD
SWEET CHAR
A New Musical Co
PRICES: Evgs. at 8:30 sharp
Dress Circle $9.50; Front Mez
Box $8.50; Rear Mezz. $7.50, 6
Mats. Wed. at 2 & Sat. at 2:3
Dress Circle $6.25; Front Mezz
Box $5.25; Rear Mezz. $4.25,
Air-Cond. PALACE B'way &

Love is when he doesn't say

"I know some people you can look up"

when you say you've been offered

a job in Paris

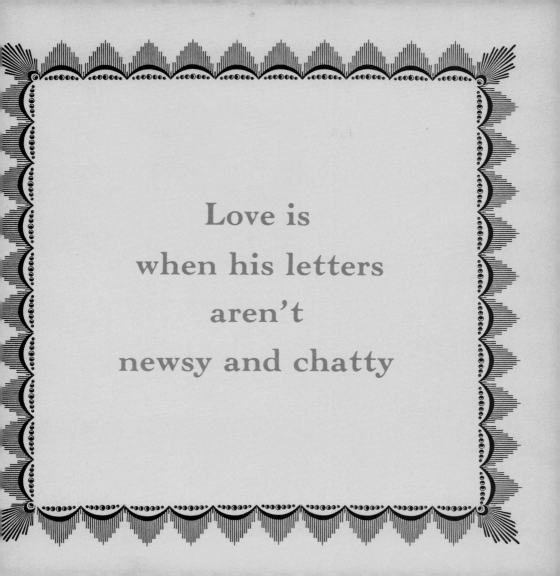

Love is
when his letters
aren't
newsy and chatty

Love is when
he wants to marry you
even though
you're in analysis

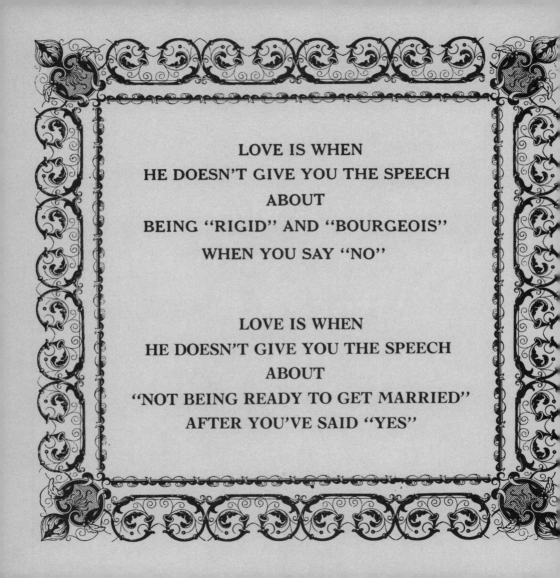

LOVE IS WHEN
HE DOESN'T GIVE YOU THE SPEECH
ABOUT
BEING "RIGID" AND "BOURGEOIS"
WHEN YOU SAY "NO"

LOVE IS WHEN
HE DOESN'T GIVE YOU THE SPEECH
ABOUT
"NOT BEING READY TO GET MARRIED"
AFTER YOU'VE SAID "YES"

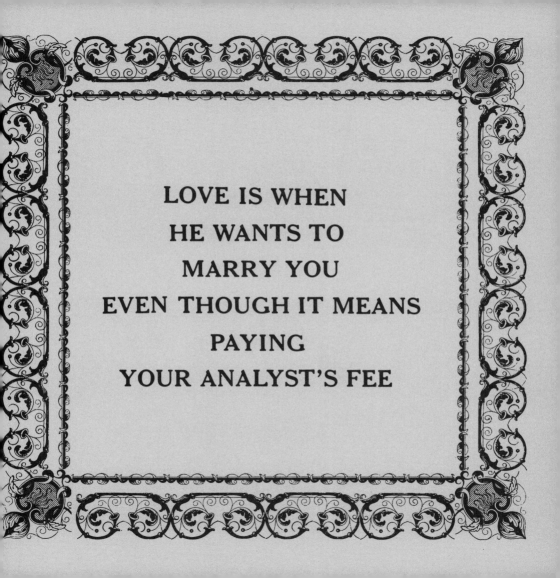

LOVE IS WHEN
HE WANTS TO
MARRY YOU
EVEN THOUGH IT MEANS
PAYING
YOUR ANALYST'S FEE

Love
is when
he doesn't go
to cocktail parties
by
himself

Love is when
he turns down
a friend's offer
to "fix him up with
a terrific girl"

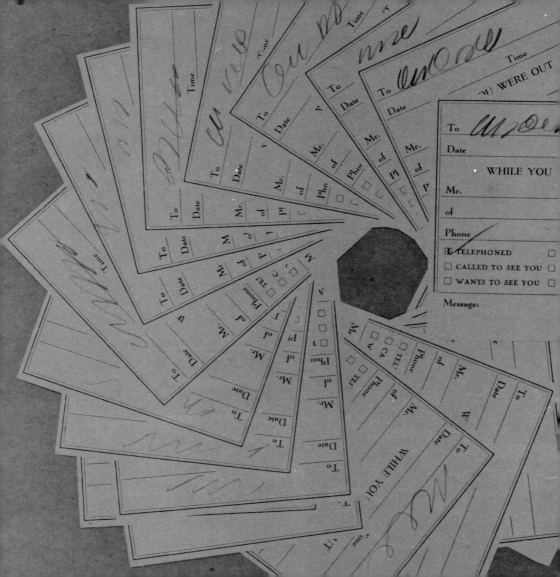

Love is when
he doesn't care
how many messages
you leave for him
at work

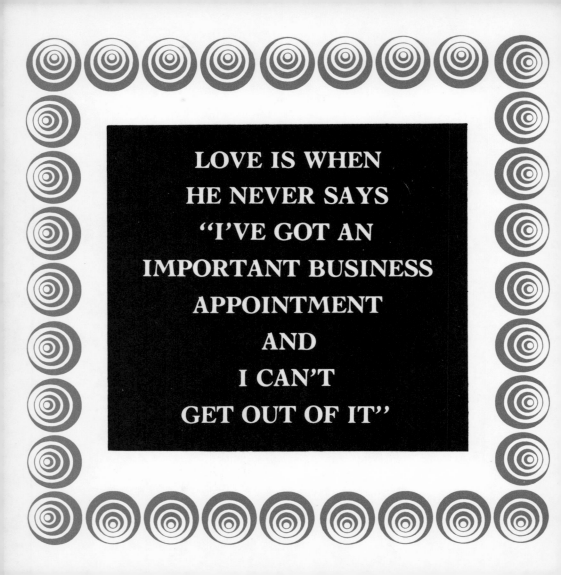

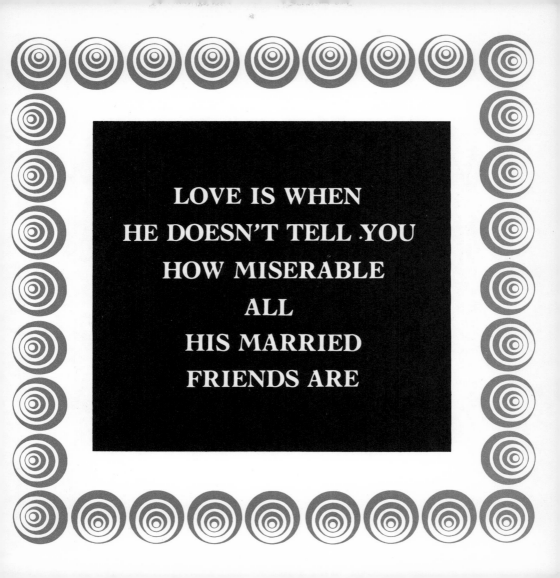

LOVE IS WHEN
HE DOESN'T TELL YOU
HOW MISERABLE
ALL
HIS MARRIED
FRIENDS ARE

Love is when he assumes the untidiness in your apartment is your roommate's fault

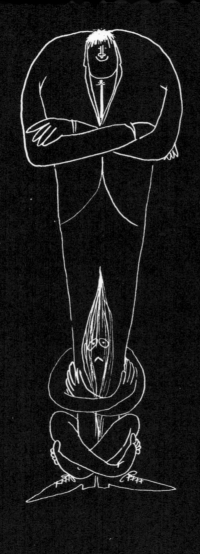

Love
is when he still wants
to marry you
even though his psychiatrist
says you're just
dependent on him

Love is when
he still wants to marry you
after his family finds out
you have no money

Love is

when he lets you borrow his car...

when he calls you again
after you've dented his car...

when he doesn't show any
resentment because you won't
let him drive your car

Love is
when he still
wants you after
an Old Flame
decides she loves
him after all

dive

Love is when he says his
wife doesn't understand him—
and gets a divorce!

rce

Love is when
he doesn't panic
in front of
furniture
store
windows

Love is when
you are desirable to him
even though
you
haven't been married
and divorced

LOVE IS WHEN
HE GIVES YOU
THE GREEN
STAMPS HE'S
BEEN SAVING
FOR SEVEN
YEARS

Love is when he offers marriage, instead of help, when you say you're looking for a new apartment

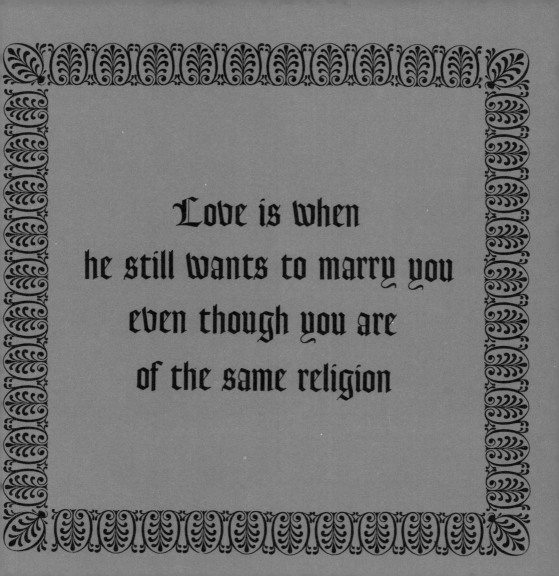

Love is when
he still wants to marry you
even though you are
of the same religion

Love is when
he wants to marry you
even though
his mother is still well
and strong

Love is when
he wants to go through
with the wedding after
your families have met

LOVE IS
WHEN HE DOESN'T
DISAPPEAR
AFTER SEEING YOU
EVERY NIGHT FOR
THREE WEEKS

LOVE IS

WHEN HE DOESN'T

DISAPPEAR

PUBLISHED BY

PRICE
STERN
SLOAN